M000032115

Forever Grateful To You:

____

____

____

[illegible]

[illegible]

[illegible]

[illegible]

Made in the USA
Monee, IL
08 March 2023

29416721R00066